Alex W. Abell

By-Laws of Oakland Lodge, No. 188, of free and accepted

Masons

Alex W. Abell

By-Laws of Oakland Lodge, No. 188, of free and accepted Masons

ISBN/EAN: 9783337146160

Printed in Europe, USA, Canada, Australia, Japan

Cover: Foto ©ninafisch / pixelio.de

More available books at **www.hansebooks.com**

BY-LAWS

OF

OAKLAND LODGE, No. 188,

OF

Free and Accepted Masons,

HELD AT OAKLAND, CAL.

Being the Uniform Code recommended by the Grand Lodge at
its Annual Communication, A. L. 5860 ;

WITH

THE FUNERAL SERVICE,

AS ARRANGED BY

THE V∴W∴BRO. ALEX. W. ABELL,

Grand Secretary of the Grand Lodge of California;

AND A

FUNERAL DIRGE AND OTHER ODES.

Stated Meetings first Wednesday of each month.

OAKLAND:

OAKLAND DAILY NEWS BOOK AND JOB PRINT.

1869.

OFFICERS

OF

Oakland Lodge, No. 188, F. & A. M.

DECEMBER, A. L. 5868.

NATHAN W. SPAULDING.................Master.
J. B. SCOTCHLER.....................Sen. Warden.
E. H. PARDEE.......................Jun. Warden.
L. G. CHAPMAN......................Treasurer.
CHAS. B. RUTHERFORD................Secretary.
W. A. PARKINSON....................Sen. Deacon.
A. W. HAWKETT......................Jun. Deacon.
F. REICHLING.......................Marshal.
B. F. STILLWELL....................⎫
JAS. H. WILSON.....................⎬ Stewards.
G. R. WALKER.......................Tyler.

BY-LAWS.

ARTICLE I.

OF NAME AND OFFICERS.

SECTION 1. This Lodge shall be known by the name of OAKLAND LODGE, No. 188, of Free and Accepted Masons ; and its officers shall consist of a Master, a Senior Warden, a Junior Warden, a Treasurer, a Secretary, a Senior Deacon, a Junior Deacon, a Marshal, two Stewards, a Tyler, and such other officers as the Lodge may deem proper to appoint.

ARTICLE II.

OF ELECTIONS AND APPOINTMENTS.

SECTION 1. The Master, the Senior and Junior Wardens, the Treasurer, and the Secretary, shall be elected by ballot, in conformity with Section 1, Article 1, Part IV, of the Constitution* of the Grand Lodge. The other officers shall be appointed by the Master, except the Junior Deacon, who may be appointed by the Senior Warden.

ARTICLE III.

OF MEETINGS OF THE LODGE.

SECTION 1. The stated meetings of this Lodge shall

be holden on the first Wednesday in each month, commencing at $7\frac{1}{2}$ o'clock, P.M., from October 1st to March 1st, and at 8 o'clock, P.M., during the remainder of the year.

SEC. 2. Special meetings may be called from time to time, as the Lodge or the presiding officer thereof may direct.

ARTICLE IV.

OF INITIATION AND MEMBERSHIP.

SECTION 1. All petitions for initiation or affiliation must be signed by the petitioner, and be recommended by two members of the Lodge. Every such petition shall be referred to a committee of three, whose duty it shall be to report thereon at the next stated meeting (unless further time be granted), when the applicant may be balloted for, and received or rejected, or the ballot may be postponed until the ensuing stated meeting, as the Lodge may determine.

SEC. 2. If any applicant, elected to receive the degrees in this Lodge, does not come forward to be initiated within three months thereafter, the fee shall be forfeited, unless the Lodge shall otherwise direct.

SEC. 3. Every person raised to the degree of Master Mason in, or elected a member of, this Lodge, shall sign the By-Laws thereof.

ARTICLE V.

OF THE TREASURER.

SECTION 1. The Treasurer shall receive all moneys from the Secretary; shall keep an accurate and just account thereof; and shall pay the same out only upon an order duly signed by the Master, and countersigned by the Secretary. He shall, at the stated meetings in June and December of each year, submit a report in full of the monetary transactions of the Lodge. The Lodge may also, at any time when considered necessary, cause him to present an account of his receipts and disbursements, and of the amount of funds on hand.

SEC. 2. He shall, if required by the Lodge, execute a good and sufficient bond to the Master for the faithful performance of his duties.

ARTICLE VI.

OF THE SECRETARY.

SECTION 1. The Secretary shall keep a faithful record of all proceedings proper to be written; shall transmit a copy of the same to the Grand Lodge, when required; shall keep a separate account for each member of the Lodge; shall report at the stated meetings in June and December, the amounts due by each; shall receive all moneys due the Lodge, and pay the same to the Treasurer; and shall perform all such other duties as may properly appertain to his office.

SEC. 2. He shall receive such compensation for his services as the Lodge may direct.

ARTICLE VII.

OF THE TYLER.

SECTION 1.   The Tyler, in addition to the necessary duties of his office, shall serve all notices and summonses, and perform such other services as may be required of him by the Lodge.

SEC. 2.   He shall receive such compensation for his services as the Lodge may direct.

ARTICLE VIII.

OF FEES.

SECTION 1.   The table of fees for this Lodge shall be as follows :   ·

To accompany the Petition, . . .	$30.00
Before taking the First Degree, . .	20.00
Total for the Three Degrees, .	$50.00
For Affiliation, :	5.00

ARTICLE IX.

OF DUES.

SECTION 1.   The dues of each member of this Lodge shall be one dollar per month, payable quarterly in advance.

SEC. 2.   No member who shall be in arrears for dues at the time of the annual election, shall be permitted to vote, or shall be eligible to any office.

SEC. 3.   Any member who shall have been suspended for non-payment of his dues shall be restored to membership upon payment of all arrearages.

SEC. 4. Any member in good standing may withdraw from membership by paying his dues and notifying the Lodge to that effect at a stated meeting ; but no recommendatory certificate shall be issued unless ordered by the Lodge.

SECTION 5. Any member may become a life member of this Lodge by paying to the Lodge the sum of one hundred dollars, and should such life members wish to demit, he shall be, entitled to fifty per cent of the original amount paid. But in case of the death of such a life member his widow or orphans shall be entitled to the whole amount paid in.

ARTICLE X.

OF COMMITTEES.

SECTION 1. The Master and Wardens shall be a Charity Committee, and shall have power to draw upon the Treasurer for any sum not exceeding twenty-five dollars at any one time, for the relief of a distressed worthy brother, his wife, widow or orphans.

SEC. 2. The Master, at the stated meeting next succeeding his installation, shall appoint an auditing committee, whose duty it shall be to examine all accounts presented against the Lodge.

SEC 3. All reports of committees shall be made in writing.

ARTICLE XI.

OF REVEALING THE TRANSACTIONS OF THE LODGE.

SECTION 1. When a candidate for initiation or affiliation is rejected, or a brother reprimanded, suspended, or expelled, no member or visitor shall reveal, either directly or indirectly, to such persons, or to any other, any transactions which may have taken place on the subject; nor shall any proceeding of the Lodge, not proper to be made public, be disclosed outside thereof, under the penalty of reprimand, suspension, or expulsion, as the Lodge may determine.

ARTICLE XII.

OF THE ORDER OF BUSINESS.

SECTION 1. The regular order of business, at every stated meeting of this Lodge, shall be as follows:

1. Reading the Minutes.
2. Reports of Committees.
3. Ballotings.
4. Reception of Petitions.
5. Miscellaneous and Unfinished Business.
6. Conferring Degrees.

ARTICLE XIII.

OF AMENDMENTS.

SECTION 1. These By-Laws, so far as relates to the time of meeting, and the amount of fees, dues, and disbursements by the charity committee, may be amended at any stated meeting, by the votes of two-thirds of the members present; *provided*, that notice of such amendment shall have been given at·the stated meeting next preceeding ; but such amendment shall have no effect until approved by the Grand Lodge or Grand Master, and until such approval shall have been transmitted to the Grand Secretary.

EXTRACT FROM SEC. 9, ART. III, PART III, OF GRAND LODGE CONSTITUTION.

"No Lodge shall expel a member for the nonpayment of his dues ; but in case any member shall have refused or neglected to pay his regular dues during a period of six months, he shall be notified that, unless at the next stated meeting, either his dues be paid, or sickness or inability to pay be shown as the cause of such refusal or neglect, he will be suspended from all the rights and privileges of Masonry. If neither of these things be done, he shall be so suspended, unless, for special reasons shown, the Lodge may otherwise determine: but any Mason thus suspended, who shall at any time pay the arrearages due at the time of his suspension, together with such further dues as would, had he retained his membership, have accrued against him to the date of such payment, shall by that act be restored."

EXTRACT FROM ART. 11, PART VII, OF GRAND LODGE CONSTITUTION.

"The suspension of a Mason is a temporary deprivation of all his rights and privileges as such, and prohibits all Masons and Lodges from holding any Masonic intercourse whatever with him, until he shall be legally restored by the Lodge which suspended him, or by the Grand Lodge."

EXTRACT FROM GENERAL REGULATIONS OF GRAND LODGE.

"11.   All Masons heretofore stricken from the rolls of Lodges within this jurisdiction, for nonpayment of dues, who have not been reinstated, are hereby declared to be suspended, as provided in Sec. 9, Art. III, Part III. of the new Constitution.— [*May.* 1859."]

Funeral Service.

No Mason can be interred with the formalities of the Order, unless he shall have been raised to the Third Degree. Fellow Crafts and Entered Apprentices are not entitled to Masonic obsequies, nor can they join in processions on such occasions.

All brethren in attendance at a funeral should be decently clothed in black, with crape upon the left arm, and with white gloves and aprons.

The brethren having assembled at the Lodge room, the Master opens the Lodge in the Third Degree of Masonry, and states the purpose for which it has been called together.

The service is then commenced as follows:

Master. What man is he that liveth and shall not see death? Shall he deliver his soul from the hand of the grave?

Response. Man walketh in a vain shadow; he heapeth up riches and cannot tell who shall gather them.

Master. When he dieth, he shall carry nothing away; his glory shall not descend after him.

Response. Naked came he into the world, and naked must he return.

Master. The Lord gave, and the Lord hath taken away ; blessed be the name of the Lord.

Solemn music may here be introduced, after which the Master, taking the SACRED ROLL in his hand. says

Let us die the death of the righteous, and let our last end be like theirs.

Response. God is our God for ever and ever : He will be our guide even unto death.

The Master then records the name and age of the deceased upon the roll and says :

Almighty. Father! Into Thy hands we commend the soul of our beloved brother. •

Response. (Repeated thrice, giving the Grand Honors each time.) The will of God is accomplished! So mote it be! Amen !

The Master then deposits the roll in the archives, and repeats the following prayer :

Most glorious God ! Author of all good, and Giver of all mercy ! Pour down Thy blessings upon us, we beseech Thee, and strengthen our solemn engagements with the ties of sincere affection ! Endow us with fortitude and resignation in this our dark hour of sorrow, and grant that this afflicting dispensation from Thy hands may be sanctified in its results upon the hearts of those who now meet here to mourn ! May the present instance of mortality remind us of our approaching fate, and draw our attention towards Thee, the only refuge in time of need ; that when the awful moment shall arrive at which we. too, must quit this transitory scene, the enlivening prospect of Thy mercy may dispel the gloom of death,

and that, after our departure hence, in peace and in
Thy favor, we may be received into Thy everlasting
kingdom, to enjoy the just reward of a virtuous and
pious life. Amen.

Response. So mote it be!

Solemn music may here again be introduced, during
which a procession is formed. If the body be not in
the Lodge room, the procession will move to the
house of the deceased, and thence with his remains
to the place of sepulture, in the following order :

The Tyler, with a drawn sword ;

Stewards, with white Rods ;

Musicians ;

(If Masons, otherwise they will follow the Tyler ;)

Master Masons ;

Junior and Senior Deacons :

Secretary and Treasurer ;

Junior and Senior Wardens ;

Past Masters ;

The Holy Writings ;

(On a cushion covered with black cloth, carried by the
oldest member of the Lodge ;)

The Master ;

The Reverend Clergy :

The   Body,

With the Insignia   placed thereon ;

Pall Bearers :   Pall Bearers :

Mourners.

The Brethren should not leave their places during the procession. Upon arriving at the place of burial, the members of the Lodge will form a circle around the grave ; the clergyman and officers of the Lodge will proceed to its head, and the mourners will be placed at its foot. The services will then be resumed by the Master, as follows :

Once more, my Brethren, have we assembled to perform the last sad and solemn duties to the dead. The mournful notes which betoken the departure of a spirit from its earthly tabernacle have again alarmed our outer door, and another has been taken to swell the numbers in that unknown land whither our fathers have gone before us.

Our Brother has reached the end of life. The brittle thread which bound him to earth has been severed, and the liberated spirit has winged its flight to the unknown world. The silver cord is loosed ; the golden bowl is broken : the pitcher is broken at the fountain, and the wheel is broken at the cistern. The dust has returned to the earth as it was, and the spirit has returned to God who gave it.

While we deplore the loss of our beloved Brother, and pay this fraternal tribute to his memory, let us not forget, my Brethren, that we, too, are mortal ; that our bodies, now so strong and vigorous, must ere long, like his, become tenants of the narrow grave ; and that our spirits, too, like his, must return to the God who spake them into existence : " Man that is born of a woman is of few days, and full of trouble. He cometh forth as a flower, and is cut down: he fleeth also as a shadow, and continueth not." The Almighty *fiat* has gone forth—"Dust thou art, and unto dust shalt thou return;"—and that we are all subject to that dread decree, the solemn cause of our present meeting, the daily observation of our lives, and the mournful mounds which indicate this population of the dead, furnish evidence not to be forgotten.

Seeing, then, my Brethren, that life is so uncertain, and that all earthly pursuits are vain, let us no longer postpone the all-important concern of preparing for eternity; but let us embrace the present moment, while time and opportunity are offered, to provide against that great change when all the pomps and pleasures of this fleeting world will pall upon the sense, and the recollection of a virtuous and well spent life will yield the only comfort and consolation. Thus we shall not be hurried, unprepared, into the presence of that all-wise and powerful Judge, to whom the secrets of all hearts are known; and on the great day of reckoning we shall be ready to give a good account of our stewardship while here on earth.

With becoming reverence, then, let us supplicate the Divine Grace to insure the favor of that eternal Being whose goodness and power know no bounds; that, on the arrival of that momentous hour when the fading taper of human life shall faintly glimmer in the socket of existence, our faith may remove the dark shroud, draw aside the sable curtains of the tomb, and bid Hope sustain and cheer the departing spirit.

This city of the dead, my Brethren, has an overwhelming emphasis in its solemn silence. It tells us of the gathering, within its embrace, of the parents' fondest hopes ;' of the disseverance of all earthly ties to the departed ones who gave us birth ; of the darkness into which the bright prospects of the loving husband and the devoted wife have suddenly been engulphed ; of the unavailing grief of the affectionate brother and tender sister ; of the dread sleep of death which here envelopes the subject of many an early, many an instantaneous call into eternity, given in the midst of health, of gayety, and of brighest hopes.

And our departed Brother, where is he? All that remains of him here on earth is now enclosed in that narrow coffin, a lifeless mass of clay. The deep, the agonizing sorrow of those to whom he was most near and dear—the scalding tears which have been shed upon his last earthly tenement—the manly and fraternal grief of his brethren of the Mystic tie — are all by him unheeded. His every faculty has fled: the purple current which sustained his life has ceased to flow ; the tongue, which was wont to give utterance to the emotions and feelings of the heart, performs no more its functions ; the eyes, which so late reflected the movements of the intelligent principle within, are now closed in death ; unfitted to remain longer upon the earth, we lay him reverently beneath its surface.   A little narrow spot is all that he now can fill ; the clod will hide him from our view, and the places which have known him here, will known him no more forever.

We consign him to the grave—to the long sleep of death ; and so profound will be that sleep that the giant tread of the earthquake, even, shall not disturb it.   There will be slumber until the Arch- angel's trump shall usher in that eventful morn, when, by our Supreme Grand Master's word, he will be raised to that blissful Lodge which no time can remove, and which, to those worthy of admission, will remain open during the boundless ages of eternity. In that Heavenly Sanctuary, the Mystic Light un- mingled with darkness, will reign unbroken and per- petual.   There, amid the sunbeam smiles of Immu- table Love, under the benignant bend of the All- Seeing Eye, in that temple, not made with hands, eternal in the heavens—there, my Brethren, may Almighty God of His infinite mercy, grant that we may finally meet to part no more.

The following invocations are then rehearsed by the Master and responded to by the Brethren.

Master.   May we be true and faithful, and may we live and die in love !

Response.   So mote it be !

Master.   May we profess only that which is good, and may we always act in accordance with our pro- fessions !

Response.   So mote it be !

Master. May the Lord bless us and prosper us, and may all our good intentions be crowned with success!

Response. So mote it be!

Master. Glory be to God in the highest! on earth peace and good will toward men.

Response. So mote it be, now, henceforth, and for-evermore. Amen!

The apron is then taken from the coffin and handed to the Master ; the coffin is deposited in the grave ; and the Master continues :

This Lambskin, or white apron, is an emblem of innocence, and the peculiar badge of a Mason. It is more ancient than the Golden Fleece or Roman Eagle, and, when worthily worn, more honorable than Star or Garter, or any other order which earthly power can confer. This emblem I now deposit in the grave of our deceased Brother. (Drops it in the grave.) By this act we are reminded of the univer-sal dominion of death. The arm of Friendship can-not oppose the King of Terrors ; the shield of fraternal love cannot protect his victim ; nor can the charms of innocence avert his fatal touch. All, all must die. This grave, that coffin, and this circle of mourning friends, remind us that we too are mor-tal, and that ere long our bodies also shall moulder into dust. How important, then, it is for us to know that our Redeemer liveth, and that he shall stand at the latter day upon the earth.

(Taking the sprig of Acacia in his hand.)

This Evergreen, which once marked the temporary resting place of one illustrious in Masonic history, is an emblem of our enduring faith in the immortality of the soul. By it we are reminded that we have an immortal part within us, which shall survive the grave, and which will never, never die. By it we are admonished that, though like our Brother, whose remains now lie before us, we too shall soon be clothed in the habiliments of death, and be deposited in the silent tomb, yet, through the loving goodness of our Supreme Grand Master we may confidently hope that, like this Evergreen, our souls will hereafter flourish in eternal spring.

The Brethren here move in procession around the grave, each depositing in it a sprig of Evergreen as he passes the head. The Secretary then drops his Roll upon the coffin; and the public Grand Honors are given thrice, all repeating at each time:

The will of God is accomplished! So mote it be! Amen!

The ceremony is then continued by the Master, as follows:

From time immemorial it has been the custom, among the Fraternity of Free and Accepted Masons, at the request of a Brother, to accompany his remains to the place of interment, and there to deposit them with the usual formalities of the Craft.

In conformity to this usage, and accordance with the duty which we owe to our departed Brother, whose loss we most deeply do deplore, we have assembled in the character of Masons to offer up to his memory, before the world, the last sad tribute of our affection ; thereby demonstrating the sincerity of our past esteem for him, and our steady attachment to the principles of our beloved Order.

⌐ The Great Creator having been pleased, in His infinite wisdom, to remove our Brother from the cares and troubles of this transitory life, thus severing another link in the fraternal chain by which we are bound together—let us, who survive him, be yet more strongly cemented by the ties of union, friendship, and brotherly love ; that, during the brief space allotted to us here, we may wisely and usefully employ our time, and, in the reciprocal intercourse of wise and friendly acts, mutually promote the welfare and happiness of each other.

Unto the grave we have consigned the body of our deceased Brother—earth to earth, ashes to ashes, dust to dust—there to remain until the last trump shall sound on the resurrection morn. We can trustfully leave him in the hands of a beneficent Being who has done all things well; who is glorious in His holiness, wondrous in His power, and boundless in His goodness ; and it should only be our endeavor so to improve the solemn warning now before us, that, on the great day of account, we, too, may be found worthy to inherit the kingdom prepared for us from the foundation of the world.

To the bereaved relatives of him we mourn, who now stand heart stricken by the heavy hand which has thus been laid upon them, we have but little of this world's consolation to present. We deeply, sincerely and most affectionately sympathise with them in this afflicting dispensation ; and we put up our most fervent prayers that " He who tempers the wind to the shorn lamb," will look down with compassion upon the widow and the fatherless, in the hour of desolation, and will fold the benevolent arms of His love and protection around those who are thus bereft of their earthly stay.

The Master, or Chaplain, will then repeat the following prayer :

Almighty and Eternal God--in whom we live and move, and have our being—and before whom all men must appear at the Judgment Day, to render an account of their deeds while in this life—we, who are daily exposed to the flying shafts of death, and do now surround the grave of one who has fallen 'in our midst, do most humbly beseech Thee to impress deeply on our minds the solemnities of this day, and to grant that their remembrance may be the means of turning our thoughts from the fleeting vanities of the present world, to the lasting glories of the world to come. Let us continually be reminded of the frail tenure by which we hold our earthly existence ; that in the midst of life we are in death ; and that, however *upright* may have been our walk, and however *square* our conduct, we must all submit as victims to the great destroyer, and endure the humble *level* of the tomb. Grant us Thy divine as-

sistance, O most merciful God, to redeem our mis-
spent time; and, in the discharge of the important
duties which Thou hast assigned us in the erection
of our moral edifice, wilt Thou give us *wisdom* to direct us, *strength* to support us, and the *beauty* of holiness to adorn our labors and render them accepta-
ble in Thy sight. And when our *work* on earth is
done, and our bodies shall go down to mingle with
their kindred dust, may our immortal souls, freed
from their cumbrous clay, be received into Thy keep-
ing, to rest forever in that spiritual house, not made
with hands, eternal in the Heavens. Amen !

Response. So mote it be !

The Master then approaches the head of the grave
and says :

Soft and safe to you, my Brother, be this earthy
bed ! Bright and glorious be thy rising from it !
Fragrant be the cassia sprig that here shall flourish !
May the earliest buds of spring unfold their beau-
ties o'er this your resting place, and here may the
sweetest of the summer's last rose linger longest !
Though the cold blasts of autumn may lay them in the
dust, and for a time destroy the loveliness of their existence, yet the destruction is not final, and in the
spring they shall surely bloom again. So, in the
bright morning of the world's resurrection, your mor-
tal frame now laid in the dust by the chilling blast of
Death, shall spring again into newness of life, and
expand, in immortal beauty, in realms beyond the
skies. Until then, dear Brother, until then farewell !

(*Benediction.*) The Lord bless us and keep us—the Lord make his face to shine upon us, and be gracious unto us—the Lord lift upon us the light of his countenance, and give us peace.

Response. Amen! So mote it be.

Thus the services end. The procession will reform and return to the Lodge room, and the Lodge will be closed in the customary manner.

FUNERAL DIRGE.

Air—*Pleyel's German Hymn.*

1. Solemn strikes the fun'ral chime,
Notes of our departing time,
As we journey here below
Through a pilgrimage of woe.

2. Mortals now indulge a tear,
For mortality is here ;
See how wide her trophies wave
O'er the slumbers of the grave.

3. Here. another guest we bring !
Seraphs, of celestial wing,
To our fun'ral altar come ;
Waft a Friend and Brother home.

4. Far beyond the grave, there lie
Brighter mansions in the sky ;
Where, enthroned, the Deity
Gives man immortality.

5. There, enlarged, his soul will see
What was vailed in mystery ;
Heavenly glories of the place
Show his Maker "face to face."

6. God of Life's ETERNAL DAY!
   Guide us, lest from thee we stray
   By a false, delusive light,
   To the shades of endless night.

7. Calm, the GOOD MAN meets his fate ;
   Guards celestial round him wait !
   See ! he bursts these mortal chains,
   And o'er Death the vict'ry gains !

8. Lord of all below, above,
   Fill our souls with Truth and Love ;
   As dissolves our Earthly Tie,
   Take us to Thy LODGE ON HIGH !

NOTE.—It is customary to sing only the 1st, 3d and 8th stanzas. On funeral occasions the first two of these may be sung on entering the burial ground, while moving in procession ; and the last during the ceremonies at the grave.

A CLOSING HYMN.

A IR—*Home, Sweet Home.*

Farewell till again we shall welcome the time
Which brings us once more to our fame-cherished
    shrine ;
And though from each other we distant may roam,
Again may all meet in this, our dear loved home :
    Home, home—sweet, sweet home ;
May every dear Brother find joy and peace at home.

And when our last parting on earth shall draw nigh,
And we shall be called to the Grand Lodge on high,
May each be prepared, when the summons shall come,
To meet the Grand Master in Heaven, our Home :
    Home, home—sweet, sweet home ;
May every dear Brother in Heaven find a home.

ODE FOR THE THIRD DEGREE.

Air— *Pleyel's German Hymn.*

1. Ah! when shall we three meet like them,
Who last were at Jerusalem?
For three there were, and one is not—
He lies where Cassia marks the spot.

2. Though poor he was, with kings he trod:
Though great, he humbly knelt to God;
Ah! when shall those restore again
The broken links of Friendship's chain?

3. Behold! where mourning Beauty bent
In silence o'er his monument,
And wildly spread in sorrow there,
The ringlets of the flowing hair!

4. The future sons of grief shall sigh,
While standing round in Mystic Tie,
And raise their hands, alas! to Heaven,
In anguish that no hope is given.

5. From whence we came, or whither go,
Ask me no more, nor seek to know,
Till three shall meet, who formed, like them,
The Grand Lodge at Jerusalem.

FORMATION OF OAKLAND LODGE, No. 188,
ᵞ F. & A. M.

MARCH 7, 1868.

The following named Brethren met at the Hall of Live Oak Lodge, in the City of Oakland, for the purpose of petitioning Wm. A. Davies, the Grand Master of the State of California, for a dispensation to form a new Lodge, to be known as OAKLAND LODGE, F. & A. M. :

NATHAN W. SPAULDING,	form'ly of	Mission Lodge, No. 169,
JOSEPH W. HOAG,	formerly of	Live Oak Lodge, No. 61,
ENOCH H. PARDEE,	"	Excelsior Lodge, No. 166,
GEORGE R. WALKER,	"	Mount Moriah Lodge, 44,
JOHN W. MYRICK,	"	Rising Star, No. 83,
CHAS. B. RUTHERFORD,	"	Tuolumne Lodge, No. 3,
ARTHUR W. HAWKETT,	"	Live Oak Lodge, No. 61,
WM. C. HOAGLAND,	"	Naval Lodge, No. 87,
JOHN LAING,	"	Live Oak Lodge, No. 61,
WILLIAM H. SMITH,	"	Warren Lodge, No. 147.
PERRY JOHNSON,	"	Live Oak Lodge, No. 61,
JOHN HILL,	"	Victoria, No. 783, B. C.
FRANCIS REICHLING,	"	Volcano Lodge, No. 56.

Whose names appeared in the Dispensation, and comprise the Charter Members of Oakland Lodge. After the transaction of the necessary business, the meeting adjourned, to await the action of the Grand Master, and to assemble at the call of the Chairman. On March 18th, 1868, the above named brethren reassembled at the call of Bro. Nathan W. Spaulding, the appointed Master of the new Lodge under dispensation, who stated that their prayer for a dispensation had been granted, and that all the necessary documents for the formation of a Lodge were now in his possession.

After the reading of the Dispensation, bearing date March 16th, A.L. 5868 (A.D. 1868), signed by Wm. A. Davies, Grand Master, and Alex. G. Abel, Grand Secretary, appointing Brother Nathan W. Spaulding the first Master, Bro. Joseph W. Hoag the first S. W., and Bro. Enoch H. Pardee the first J. W., the Master appointed the following Brethren to fill the several stations : Francis Reichling, Treasurer ; Charles B. Rutherford, Secretary ; L. G. Chapman, S. D. P. T.; A. W. Hawkett, J. D.; Perry Johnson and John Hill, Stewards ; G. R. Walker, Marshal ; and E. I. Smith, Tyler, P. T. After fixing the time of meetings, and the transaction of such other business as was deemed proper, the Lodge closed, to meet on Wednesday, April 1st.

The first regular meeting of Oakland Lodge was held on Wednesday Evening, April 1, 1868, at which time the first petitions were received by the Lodge for affiliation and degrees.

The next meeting was May 6th, 1868, at which time the Lodge was in full and successful operation, and balloted upon its first petitions, and commenced its labors as a working Masonic body.

On the 1st of October, 1868, the time having expired for which the Dispensation was granted, it was surrendered, and the necessary steps taken to secure from the Grand Lodge a Charter. A Charter having been granted by the Grand Lodge, bearing date October 15, A.I. 5868 (A.D. 1868). No. 188, the members met on the 4th of November, and Oakland Lodge, No. 188, was constituted and its officers installed, by Bro. Lawrence C. Owens, appointed by the Grand Master. Charles Marsh. for that purpose, assisted by Past Masters J. E. Whicher, F. Warner and Bro. James Lentell, Master of Live Oak Lodge. Bro. N. W. Spaulding was installed Master ; J. W. Hoag, S. W. ; E. H. Pardee, J. W.; F. Reichling, Treasurer ; Chas. B. Rutherford, Secretary ; L. G. Chapman. S. D.; J. W. Myrick, J. D.; Thos. Bailey and B. F. Stilwell, Stewards ; W. J. Gurnett, Marshal ; G. R. Walker, Tyler ; and E. J. Pasmore, Organist. Number of Charter Members at the organization of the Lodge, May 6th, 1868, thirteen ; number of members May 26th, 1869, eighty-nine Master Masons ; two Fellow Crafts ; six Entered Apprentices.

LIST OF MEMBERS

OF

Oakland Lodge, No. 188, F. & A. M.

May 26, 1869.

1. SPAULDING, N. W.	21. Bailey, Thos. W.
2. HOAG, J. W.	22. Gurnett, W. J.
3. PARDEE, E. H.	23. Scotchler, J. B.
4. REICHLING, F.	24. Dusenbury, M. T.
5. RUTHERFORD, CHAS. B.	25. Pasmore, E. J.
6. HAWKETT, A. W.	26. Van Wyck, John C.
7. MYRICK, J. W.	27. Snook, Wm. S.
8. WALKER, GEO. R.	28. Knowles, C. C.
9. JOHNSON, PERRY	29. Campbell, F. M.
10. HOAGLAND, WM. C.	30. Remillard, P. N.
11. HILL, JOHN	31. Wilson, Jas. H.
12. LAING, JOHN	32. Geary, Edward B.
13. SMITH, W. H.	33. Tucker, H. S.
14. Eastland, Van Leer	34. Miller, Wm. H.
15. Chapman. L. G.	35. Bartlett, Pliny
16. Tickner, Daniel	36. Larue, Jas.
17. Stilwell. B. F.	37. Parkinson, Wm. H.
18. Batchelder, Jas.	38. Webster, Jas. A.
19. Hanna. John	39. Hays, Patrick
20. McCurdy, Robert	40. Lucas, Chas. L.

41. Sessions, Edward C.
42. Adams, C. S.
43. Williams, C. S.
44. Whitney, Geo. E.
45. Reinach, E. S.
46. Phillips, M. C.
47. Matty, Chas.
48. Kelly, C. M.
49. Blethen, Jas. E.
50. Craib, Wm.
51. Heilner, S. A.
52. Smith, John F.
53. Stewart, Jas. T.
54. Smith, G. Frank
55. Harwood, W. D.
56. Greenhood, Jacob
57. Whelan, Alanson
58. Loring, Geo. Y.
59. Davenport, J. P.
60. Muscat, P. H.
61. Becht, Joseph
62. Armstrong, R. A.
63. Walker, Lysander
64. Storr, E. S.
65. Van Dyke, Walter
66. Holmes, Stillman

67. Brown, Geo. S.
68. Cook, John
69. Mann, F. A.
70. Bryant, Daniel
71. Pierson, Geo.
72. Verhave, Adrian
73. Bartling, Wm.
74. Hale, Thomas T.
75. Pratt, D. W.
76. Williams. R. N.
77. Faulkner, George L.
78. Folger, James A.
79. Briar, R. W.
80. Allardt, George F.
81. Pinkerton, Thos. H.
82. Rosenberg, N.
83. Searing, Wm. S.
84. Ward, Robert
85. Smith, E. J.
86. Kelly, Wm.
87. Doblin, Jacob
88. Terry, V. P.
89. Kipps, A. K.

FELLOW CRAFT.

1. Kilbourn, Walter L.
2. Page, Samuel

ENTERED APPRENTICES.

1. Moore, Gorham H.
2. Watson, John B.
3. Noblett, Robert

4. Ough, Richard
5. Keller, W. W.
6. Rea, Thomas

LIFE MEMBERS.

N. W. Spaulding,   Wm. Jas. Gurnett,
E. H. Pardee,   Joseph Becht,
F. Reichling,   E. S. Reinach,
G. R. Walker.   G. Frank Smith,
James Batchelder,   E. J. Pasmore,
J. B. Scotchler,   Chas. L. Lucas,
C. B. Rutherford,   F. M. Campbell,
W. H. Miller,   Walter Van Dyke.
Myron T. Dusenbury,   Thos. H. Pinkerton.